Skimming Between the Veils

the

Veils

Valerie Laub
(Theo)

Valerie Laub (Theo)

ISBN: 1727799690
ISBN-13: 978-1727799699

DEDICATION

for Misty
who preferred having her ears rubbed
to poetry
but
nevertheless….

CONTENTS

Valerie Laub (Theo)

Valerie Laub (Theo)

Perfect Ski

Cold, Cold Day

the older I get, the
more I love the
world

If a Thing is
Worth Doing....

Now, in my Sixty-
fifth Year

Healing Hands

On Turning Sixty-
Five

On Turning Sixty-
Five #2

No Matter How
Hard You Love

All This is True

Sacred Hour

twilight origami

the dog is gone

Things We Love

Skimming Between the Veils

<u>a poem begins….</u>

stone tumbling down a well

listen for a landing

nothing matters
unless everything does

never be ashamed of love

even if your first love
is an old dog
with bad breath
and a heart
that, daily, threatens to fail.

even if, after your dog,
what you love are trees.

even if you don't hug trees,
(at least, not often, and only if they ask),
but nevertheless are drawn
to wrap your arms around yourself.

then there is the sky.
this needs
no explanation.

autumn.
all the seasons, in fact.
dawn in winter —
snow so luminous, I swear
there is an incandescent seed
within.

the moments I sing true —
such a surprise!

tears that cannot simply be wiped away.

poetry galloping deep into a secret world.

The Wonder of It!

I want to tell you
how much I love the morning,
and the evening,
and the ancient, velvet night.

I want you to know about the pleasure
of walking through the woods at dawn:
sticky, piquant buds of cottonwood clinging
to the dog's paws; then
along the banks of the river,
beneath gentle peach-fuzz green
of spring alder; Canada geese
hollering overhead.

I want to describe the delight
of caressing my dog's silken ears —
her skull so fragile beneath the soft, warm fur —
even knowing that one day, and soon,
she will be gone from me.

I want to tell you about the shock
of realizing that I am growing older;
that one day, like the dog,
I will be gone.

The wonder of it!

Now, the mountain, that has been gleaming
so bright and utterly white that I could
barely raise my eyes to it,
is disappearing amid pale clouds.
Soon the day will be overcast.

I love this too.

Tidal Wave

Sometimes, walking behind my little dog,
I find myself awash in a tidal wave of tenderness —
how can any creature so small and seemingly frail
permeate such boundless space with love?

She trots along, head held high,
prodigious ears splayed like wings.
Leaping over a fallen log
she heads heavenward
but I call her back to Earth,
not ready for her to go,
not yet.

Her heart
murmurs,
thuds.
No words,
just wild
echoing
joy.

Cherish the Ache

In the night
I studied 'loneliness',
that hollow at the core of my life.

Loneliness: the very word
with it's 'o' like a black hole,
long and dominant;
the 'li' a brief moment of hope, and then,
whisked away by a mean-spirited wind,
or hidden by a wraith of mist —
'ness.'

Yes.

I was still awake when golden light started pouring
into that dark hole as if it was a portal to another
world,
or a mouth
longing for love.

trees poured in and poetry and my dog and
my aging body and....

I don't mean loneliness disappeared.
I mean I began to cherish it, cherish the ache.

Yes.

When the grey day dawned
I boiled the kettle, made tea.
The first sip burned my lips,

tasted like honey.

<u>delicate calligraphy</u>

no wind
unblinking sun
crows hunched low
rags ripped
from the breathless void

as a prairie child
I had wings
flew over fields frozen hard
feathers spilled
like blood on snow

lately I have been longing to return
stand amidst a silence that speaks

then carry on alone
cross steely snow and stubble
the rough earth clanging at every step

Thaw

Ice in the mornings.
Slush by noon.
Streets ridged with grime.

Where is our glorious winter now?
Where is the awe that spread my heart
like wings?

I know beauty must be here.
I know beauty is here —
not despite the sunken snow,
but within it.

I gaze at the grey world —
some small birds flitting about a gnarled tree;
distant pines rimed with last night's flurries;
the young birch tree that, years ago,
seeded itself by the shed,
one ragged leaf still clinging;
the pattern of its thin black branches
wavering against the sullen sky;
coppery bark faintly lined
as if with morse code,
and that one spot where the bark
is partially peeled away,
revealing new skin
the colour of sunlight —

and I dissolve,
a river of melted snow
running close
to the cherished earth.

The Dog's Dinner

I'm not much of a cook
but it looks pretty good.
If I wasn't vegetarian,
and didn't mind the odd kibble in the mix,
I would chow down beside her.

Afterwards,
she comes into my office
licking her chops,
wipes her lips
on the rug.

(Do dogs have lips?)

Then she burps.

What's not to love?

woman reclining

it was reaching out
for the mug of tea
that broke the spell.
such a simple gesture
to pull me into the world.

grey light
of a dank Saturday afternoon.
outside the window —
birch tree, skeletal at this time of year,
water dripping bone to bone.
distant cry of crows.

we expect life to be great and thundering,
yet here it is:
a grey haired woman
reclining on a red love seat,
hands wrapped around a coppery-brown mug.

Down from the Mountain

Down here the sun is soft.
Snow drips from the roofs.
Under the trees,
the frail new grass is green.

Up the mountain it was winter,
trees snow-blasted sculptures.
A different world.

We didn't go far —
snowshoed up the slope
then across the wide-open Prairie
until the world disappeared.
Nothing left
but a line of coloured jackets,

and our laughter.

I wonder what is on the other side
of nothing?

I watch my old dog,
her grizzled muzzle swaying
close to the quickening earth.

I love that she doesn't ask.

When A Tree Speaks

I wake alone.
Empty space
bowing
under a storm
long past.

Water drips leaf to leaf.

I have been told
that when a tree speaks
there is no mistaking it.

I listen. I wait. I listen.

What if, after all these years,
the tree's true tongue
is silence?

What if, in the garden,
instead of a wild rose
the bud remains a tight
pink fist?

What if all I seek
is unrecognizable
until empty space
becomes
a sacred vessel?

a thousand suns

not a slow dawn and gentle waking;
not light easing the world alive;
but out of fog and drizzle
a burst of brilliance —
dandelion erupting,
radiant seeds unleashed
across the sudden blue.

every tree
a thousand suns.

Virginia Woolf said:

something interesting happens every day

she also said:
nothing really happens until it is recorded

I pick lilacs
bring them inside

a room forms around them

a desk
a pen
a poem

a day

Sunday Afternoon

July, but the weather so cool
and changeable — rain, wind,
sun, rain — that it is too cold
to sit outside by the lake
and read or write or draw.
Even now the mountain
is disappearing.

I too am disappearing,
as if I can't exist indoors,
as if my one true home is wilderness,
and all else just a blind.

Sudden squall
blowing across the lake,
tilting the waters this way and that;
purple cloud; thick, spattering raindrops;
poplar leaves clattering;
sudden splash of sun.

Ah, here I am.

Nothing Special

Just an ordinary pond,
secreted by ferns
near the side of a trail.

A few small, tumbled trees
almost submerged;
water spiders
skimming along the still surface.

Laid across black water —
pale birch trees,
upside down;
astonishing blue sky.

Last year, just here,
I met a bear.
Both of us startled alive.
The bear reared up,
embraced a tree
as if with love.

I turned down a different path.

Every time I pass that pond
my heart gives a little hop
of happiness.

stopping beside a garden gone to weed

iris sibirica

delicate as a Japanese painting
such a surprise amidst the thistles and thorns

buds
tight pursed lips
flushed with green
veined with violet
a secret stuttered before the telling

then an unravelling of purple
a gasp of ochre
and out they stick their tigerish tongues
but not unkindly

everything is itself
everything cradles the seed
of everything else

the last time we walked by the pond
long stems undulating in the breeze
hearts breaking and mending
and breaking again
wind swaying through our temple of tenderness

when I was a child an iris
was a flower

now it is a pilgrimage

The Dog Wants....

The dog wants in.
No matter she just went out.
No matter that the sun is shining.
If she wants in I'll get up
and let her in.

It's her house after all —
I mean she lives here.
(I live here too, otherwise
who would open the door?
Who would serve her dinner?
Rub her belly?)

She has taken over the furniture.
There isn't a chair that isn't "hers."

But I don't mind.
She is elderly,
small and black, a little deaf
despite big ears, a little blind
despite eyes that are always eager,
and with a heart that can be heard at a distance.

She fills my house.
She fills my world.

That's the thing with love —
it fills whatever space it enters.
No matter what you love,
the heart of it
can be heard beating
across vast distances.

a day drenched in the sweet blessing of bees

she said
the house is filled with light

I said
I know it

fields of flowers transformed
rooms swarming gold

searing knives slide through
perfect hexagrams of honeycomb
skimming off the thinnest layer of wax
uncapping all that happiness
our hands stained bright yellow with propolis
and our lips

it could be a love story
indeed, it is

Cousins

We didn't visit them often
and my memories are sparse,
but I remember the geese and the danger
of being chased across the scraggly yard.

These cousins, a whole gaggle of them,
were poor and tough and fearless.
Dirty faces; dirty feet.

Children of the youngest sister.
The one who laughed.
The one who was loudest.
The one who married for love.

A farmer: fields of wheat, I suppose.
A few pigs, chickens, maybe a cow.
Or a goat.
Maybe.
I only remember the geese.

And I remember the cellar —
trap door into the dark;
narrow ladder
sinking beneath the floor;
damp earth smell; spider webs
thick with dust;

jars of plums, pickled beets.
Mysterious jewels.
Alluring. Frightening.

So different from tidy grocery store shelves,
the sterile city life.

Our big car, parked among the dandelions,
the crabgrass and thorns,
shimmered under the ferocious prairie sun
as my mother, simmering
in her girdle and stockings and long-line bra,
her face red as the jars of beets
in the cool cellar, unloaded boxes —
winter coats we had outgrown,
shoes we could no longer wear,
tinned corn from my father's store.

She was the oldest girl.
The one who mothered her brothers and sisters.
The one who suffered so in the Depression.
The one who married a Jew with a job.

smoke-sky

scorched

scent of failure
flat
grey

cold water
windless lake
far shore
a wan haze

disappearing

halo aflame
dive
through tea-tinged water

emerge
blue-lipped

perhaps to burn

lit from below

I long for a cottage
crouched on the moors
long nights, ferocious days
everything howling

I see myself alone
tall
spare
impossibly silent

long strides
glimmer across the heath

in the gloaming
what's lit
is lit from below

everything howling

the cottage of my longing squats low
hidden amidst flailing grasses
broken lichen-etched stone

wind-drenched
rain-shocked
blind deaf mute and tingling
I wait

dashed across a leaden sky
blackbirds sob

Love the River

In the night
I filled my pockets with rocks
and crept down to the river
of my imagination.
I thought of Virginia Woolf.
I thought of a friend who
laid herself to rest in this river
two summers before.
I thought of how there are people
who would miss me and how I would miss myself;
not wanting to die, not yet,
but afraid of the life rushing to meet me.

And so I went to the garden
because that is where my teachers are:
pansies so eager and open
you can almost hear them panting;
sunflowers who shine despite
the damp starless night;
petunias that change from fuchsia
to deep purple as they age,
darkly veined and vivid.

And I thought how the only way through
would be to love everything, everything —
to love emptiness, love fear,
love the rocks that line my pockets,
love the river.

Falling into the Light

When the universe cracked open
spirit expanded outward from within.

Once I fell off a mountain,
pulled my partner down too.

At the outer edge
of an indigo sky,
a giant moon
hugs the horizon;
the way a woman
close to spirit
is a mountain.

The two of us
falling into the light.

two peas in a pod

you write: once i thought anything
less tangible than a fence post was bullshit.

farmer, toes dug into the earth;
poet, eyes fixed on stars.

you shiver at temperatures I find searing;
I wake with delight to 40 below.

I send you photos of frost flowers;
you send me pictures of cows
with names of people and personalities
that demand I re-consider the shape of the world.

your language is rough, and your life.
you know how to mend fences,
how to save a cow with bloat.
I see you loving your land,
but loving it hard, the way a hammer
loves an anvil.

then, you tell me that one day,
kneeling there among the spinach,
cabbage white butterflies dancing around your head

like some crazy holy-day hat,
instead of breaking,
you broke open — where before,
rage flooded the parched earth,
you discovered something new —

poetry had rooted itself
in your great, thumping, open heart —

something strange as snow to a girl from the
tropics,
a girl wild from the bush.

you write: i still enjoy the integrity of fence posts,
but now my paddocks are alive with so much more.

silence within sound

how easy it is
just to listen
when the sun is warm and
the fallen apple is round and
each white bite snaps smartly
juicy and tart

sound within silence

everything essential to the damp-blue-
sun-gifted-leaf-blessed-wind-hallowed-
apple-crunching day

And Yet....

Every year, and there have been so many,
I feel the same staggering jolt
of a season snatched away.

How can this happen?

How can trees that once were vital, lime green
and cacophonous with insects, how can they now
be barren? How can leaves, lately golden and
glowing,
be dun-coloured, a wretched mat of mud
burying the earth?

Clouds plunge downward; mountains disappear.
Tiny pellets of snow pierce the feral wind.
Skeins of geese shriek across a gruelling sky.

We expect transcendence to be auspicious

and yet...
here we are —
leaning into the murky dark,

new life trembling all around.

this grey day

gold leaves flapping
red stems clinging

unbound
wheel down
saturate ochre
ground

gurgling gutters
hidden cascades
dribbling
dripping
singing
drains

How I Spend My Morning

While pouring a cup of tea
I notice a china plate
I inherited from my mother,
its delicate pattern
reflected in the smooth brown
and turquoise glaze
of a pottery bowl
I dearly love.

That takes some time.

Then my eyes are drawn outdoors —
glossy Tibetan prayer flags
wavering among the rufous leaves
of the mountain ash tree.

I take a sip of tea.

The dog, who has followed me to the kitchen,
now follows me back to the room where I write
and where my window is filled with gold —
a cottonwood tree that, years ago, chose to live
here.

I rub the dogs ears.
A crow calls.
I write a few words.
I stare out the window.
There is such fog that the world is small,
but, close by, sharp-etched, keen.

I sit in silence trying to hear
the poem unfurling
within me,
the one that begins without words,
the one that abandons time,
the one I long to live.

empty

dark days, slate skies

not a wisp of snow
to brighten the earth

above the mountain
a strip of light

six swans flying low

life is slow, almost silent
time enough for wings to rise, fall

how can life so empty
be so full?

this fearful passage

as always,
my hands are tinged with blue.

frost limns the leaves.

birch poplar dogwood rowan
yellow ochre rufous rust

overhead
cloud-rapt
black boughs
crack
a grey sky

Beloved Immortal

She sleeps harder now,
curled up with her eyes screwed tight.
She doesn't hear me when I leave the room
but soon enough comes searching.
I call and clap my hands —
even so she startles to discover
that I am standing at her side.

She follows me everywhere.
Where I am is where she wants to be.
I am honoured even if it means
cooking is fraught with peril.

She has a wobble and a shake
that shudders right through her.
Sometimes she coughs until she collapses.
But, every time, she rises
like the phoenix.

So far.

I expected her to die a year ago, two.
Now I say, 'I think she is immortal.'
What I mean is
one day she won't be here.

What I mean is
I don't know how I'll live without her.

one leaf, persevering

just outside my window,
tucked in between the house and the shed,
what used to be nothing
but gravel and weeds
is now a little forest.

against the sad shades of winter
one tree glows, coppery, stippled,
and, where the bark has peeled away,
the colour of delicate flesh, laid bare.

this tree has far out-stripped me:
grown like a weed,
galloping toward the sky —
you can almost hear hoof beats.

I love that trees have seeded themselves
here, all choosing this unlikely ground —
even the little pines pressed right against the shed,
even the mountain ash that insists on growing
through the open window.
they do not judge the soil —
they'll send their roots through rock if need be.

the air rings, quivers with cold.
one leaf, silhouetted
against the deepening twilight,
perseveres.

not a breath of wind.

What is the Source of Joy?

I wake in the inky mornings
awash with delight,
as if I spent the dark hours
immersed in kindness.

I love the frost flowers
on the window pane;
the frigid air billowing in
as I poke my head out
to check for stars,
to admire the hedge,
sculpted, as it is,
into gargoyles of snow.

Then I open my bedroom door
hoping the dog is still alive —
the little black dog with the big ears
who is growing old, and hums,
and must sit on my lap,
and must have her ears rubbed,
and must be given treats.

I love our dawn walks
with the icy-blue sky turning
pink behind the black pine trees,
above the white roofs.

I love the crunch of cold beneath my feet;
the cacophony of crows
returning from their night-time roost,
black wings sweeping across the infinite sky.
I like the yellow windows of the houses,
wondering who lives there and how.

My own life is simple,
small but deep —
if gratitude is simple,
if beauty is small,
if love is deep.

Snow Angels

I had thought that today
I might try to accomplish something sensible,
something worthwhile,
something I could point to and say,
"There!"

But with sunshine laid across the hedge like lace,
the golden yard stippled with blue shadows,
the spruce trees across the road
offering to rock me in sunlight
and asking nothing in return —
I have fallen into my day
the way children fall
onto the pillowed earth,
arms spread like wings.

spaciousness

is found in small places:
a moment,
a look,
a leaf.

clouds move across the mountain.
rivers freeze, rear up, thaw.
I sit at my desk:
brown mug still warm
after the tea is gone.

hands an empty cup.

poetry has left me

empty space crammed with words
that neglect silence,
neglect the shape of a soul.

slate sky,
snowflakes only visible
against dark pines, fissures
in the fabric of the world.

I want so much:
whole days of nothing but winter light;
snow burning the tongue;
the passion of one red berry
clinging to a branch of the mountain ash.

sometimes, when lakes freeze,
water wells up under the snow.
you don't know if you are drowning
or freezing or slipping through a portal
into another world.

hieroglyphs

such delicate snowfall
lips graze an icy cheek

two crows
dive to earth
wheel away
some great secret
grasped in keen black beaks

inky wings write
across the welkin grey

mother tongue

iron-clad winter.
everything clasped tight.
a few crinkled leaves
still loving their twigs.

roots thrum through gelid earth.

at the centre
an ancient ear.

Full Moon Dream

Such life force
emanated from the palms of my hands
that I wept with wonder.

Behind the black pine trees, dawn
the colour of lapis lazuli.

River frozen so hard
we waltzed on water
with perfect freedom.

Well out from shore
the river ran open,
inky blue and swaggering.
My dog and I, poised
on chunks of stony snow,
stared at ice
crinkled across shallow water
like transparent cloth.

Beneath the surface
rocks opened their mouths to sing.

Christmas Eve Day

Cold. Too cold for the dog
who is old, and is dying,
but not yet, not today.

Even the little apple tree, that this year
produced six fine apples,
stands blue before the hedge
with its billows of snow.
It is so still.
Everything frosted, frozen.

Alone, by the river at dawn,
I witnessed the moment
when the ice stopped flowing;
stopped it's mad susurration and
was suddenly, shockingly silent.
Nothing moved. Ice along the shore
groaned and cracked. But the channel
that had moved so swiftly moments before
stopped
and the river froze over.

Winter is such a wonder.
These precious days
of long darkness
when the veil between worlds

is gossamer-thin; when I wake
in the forever-night to angels,
and long to tell them
how the love they seeded in me
has grown into a joy
that splits my chest open —

the way a dog, even an old dog,
revels in her life;
the way a tree, so silent all the winter,
blossoms with fruit come summer;
the way a river flows on
beneath the still, silent surface.

Perfect Ski

Pristine snow; trees sculpted;
the sky shifting from grey to azure.

I ski the hills backwards, and forwards, and
backwards again. I ski around the lake to the left.
I ski around the lake to the right.
I ski the corkscrew
over and over
and over.

The whole time
smiling so hard
I have to be grateful
it is not mosquito season.

Some would call it endorphins.
But the amazing thing, the really wonderful thing,
is how it fills me with love; how elation spills over
like cream from the top of a frozen milk bottle.

Maybe it is endorphins, but if it is,
then endorphins are rich and buttery
and beg to fill me with delight.

Cold, Cold Day

So cold the little dog
manages half a block and then,
as fast as her weathered old heart allows,
bolts for home.
I lurch after her,
swaddled in an arctic jacket,
feet jammed in leaden boots.

It is important that I keep up —
after all, she can't open the door
and I know her extremities are freezing.
Once inside
I hold her ears the way,
when we were children,
our mother would hold
our aching toes.

Then, as a treat,
I give her some desiccated liver,
(not something our mother would do,
thank goodness),
and I go back out, alone,
down to the mad jumble of ice
that was once a river:
trees spiked with hoar-frost;
steam spewing from open channels.

Under a lilac sky mountain peaks are dead white.
To many it would seem a frozen hell.

But I love the cold.
I love having to check that my extremities
are coursing with hot red blood.

I love rejoicing in my own vitality
before it is my turn to follow the dog
to the very ice edge
of the abyss.

the older I get, the more I love the world

mountain ash trees
setting themselves aflame with rapture;
scent of high bush cranberry sharp as nails;
purple clouds torn open
as if by angels desperate to sing hallelujah,
their wings feathered across the open blue.

the Earth revolving and revolving and
revolving

If a Thing is Worth Doing….

Last night at my tap dancing class
I had a Shirley Temple moment —
flying down the length of the hall
with my arms flung wide….
I swear my hair turned to ringlets.

I never expected, ever, to take tap dancing lessons.
Just like I never expected to grow old
or go blind in one eye.
Come to think of it,
I never expected I'd die either.

But I will.
One day.

Meanwhile
my skin thins,
grows papery.

I am so much closer now.

Pain leaves it's mark —
bear claws on birch bark;

sap seeping down the surface,
hieroglyphs of sorrow,
yours, mine.

But if pain leaves it's mark, so does joy.
Oh! my feet tapping with it,
my heart thumping!

The freedom of believing that
if a thing is worth doing,
it is worth doing badly.

I fly down the floor just slightly out of step.
I close my good eye to check the progress
of it's weaker partner — yup, I can still see.

The autumn leaves are brilliant this year.

Now, in my Sixty-fifth Year

I am learning to play the violin.

The dog begs to be let outside.
You can imagine….

But I love it.
I mean the learning.
I mean being sixty-four and willing
to try something new
and difficult.
I love cradling that curved body,
resting my cheek against its coppery-coloured
wood.
I love striving to draw the bow
across the strings and find music.
I want to be able to close my eyes
and sway to a sweet sound,
to touch silence all around the notes.
Imagine!

When I watch a violinist
who is truly great
and see their fingers fly
and their bow move
like the wings of a hummingbird
I start to cry.
Even to think of it brings tears.
I don't know why.

Did I, all my life, yearn
to play the violin
and not discover it until now?

Perhaps I had to wait until
all that mattered was the challenge,
the yearning,
the love.

Healing Hands

My hands
used to be strong, slender, shapely.
Now they are swollen, sore,
discoloured as spoiled meat.

One day,
my hands may no longer be able
to hold the violin;
so for that very reason
I lift that elegant body to my cheek
and watch, intently,
as my fingers
stumble over the strings,
eager to sing. They are clumsy,
uncertain, a little shy.

I offer them encouragement:
I say I see them as butterflies,
their hopeful wings
opening and closing
as they rise, fall.

Instead of counting out the beat
I whisper:

thank you,
thank you,
I love you,
you are beautiful.

On Turning Sixty-Five

It's not as if I expect to die
yet
but now that I am closing in on sixty-five
I do expect to die.

Such a surprising gift.

I step out into my backyard,
darkening sky blue, mottled;
snow piled high all around.
I am in awe:
I live here, here —
the eaves of my house
lined with icicles — not a good sign
but they are beautiful,
shaped by shadow and light.

So ordinary.
So miraculous.

Beneath snow clad pines,
a deer stands, ears alert,
staring.

On Turning Sixty-Five #2

I am pleased, proud.
Relieved, I suppose —
I've made it this far,
too late to die young.

Oh course, it is possible
that I will die piecemeal, overcome by pain
or loneliness; embittered by all that loss.
Or my mind might turn away from the world,
erase me while I am still breathing.

At least I'm here now,

aware of the way
everything is layered, everything enlarged
by memories I can't quite recall.
I look at the sky spilling snow
over the grey world
and what comes back
is some happiness —
the colour of a distant light shining
at dusk; or I hear a single note ringing
and sorrow flings me backwards,
arms spread like angel wings.

Looking up I find
my whole life etched
across a cloud-strewn sky.
I feel so rich.

I know, one day,
I'll have to go.

All I'll leave behind
is what I've loved.

No Matter How Hard You Love

Outside the office window
it is grey, the mountain that towers
over our town is swathed in cloud.

So I move into the living room to write.
The window faces east and in this direction
the sun is rising, there are yellow clouds
flung across an encouraging sky,
and although I cannot see them
above the snow-covered hedge
and the trees that rise up across the road
like thin hurrahs of ink,
there are mountains.

Earlier, out walking,
the sun had splashed the sky
with gentle coral pinks and mauves.
Despite the bitter wind the sky itself
was the colour of summer.
I heard a bird sing and that little voice
brought it all back — the seasons,
that they'll pass, no matter how hard
you love them.

It made me think of my little old dog
who, day-by-day, totters a little closer to death.
It makes me think of my own aging.
And of my mother, who, at my age,
lost her mind.

You can do what you can do
but really, you are still going to die.

And so I choose the living room window,
drawing the day into a poem that reminds me
death is also a window. One day,
it will swing wide open.

All This is True

It was a rare cold and starlit night.
Now, in the early morning,
although it looks kind —
so soft is the gold light,
so rounded the blue shadows —
the snow is abrasive, frozen steely as stone.
Even the river has cracked open.

Later today the snow will melt,
collapse in on itself.
With every step you will sink to your knees.

Such unseasonable warmth.

End of February.
Weather for the end of March.
Already trees sing at sunrise.

It is lovely, disappointing, frightening.
February is meant to be unfathomable winter.
So much depends upon it.

And yet all this is true:
stars, soft shadows,
the river running.

In the brilliant light
the mountain is knife-edged,
sharp-shadowed,
unforgiving,

beautiful.

Sacred Hour

I sit before the window,
as I do every evening,
watching the day turn blue,
watching trees march into darkness
and disappear.

Moment by moment paintings
appear on the snowy hedge.
Moment by moment I appear,
a ghost of light
among the branches,
wondering without words.

When I step into the garden
everything has turned inside-out,
a photographic negative:
white branches, black sky.
Stars ringing.

Through the window
the empty room glows.

twilight origami

sun disappears behind the mountain.
cold intensifies, turns blue,
folds light into an origami of awe.

above the ridge the sky is pale,
lit from below.

mountain in winter:
massive silence,
deep-throated,
shuddering.
roar without sound.

all the while
light is soaring
to the other side of the world.

the dog is gone

she taught me to love.
spread my heart wide
and nested there.

now the tendrils of our tenderness
float free,
gossamer threads
seeking something to hold close.

this terrible, natural, inevitable,
unbelievably final loss.

I walk through the house
where I have almost never been
without her at my side
wailing, "Where is she?
Where is she?"

she left
just as the sandhill cranes were returning,
angel laughter
spread across the skies.

tulips I forgot
I ever planted

rising
through the snow
of a long winter.

that night
a single star
burned bright
through my open window.

Things We Love

When I look
to the peak above our town
the surface is glazed;
every ridge and cornice etched
as if with acid —
shadows that sharp.

Then, a film of cloud —
and the mountain steps back,
disappearing.

So it is with things we love —
winter; mountains; each other.

We start from a shining so clear
it hurts the eyes; then, things soften,
sky and mountains merge.
We barely recognize ourselves.
Our dreams become foreign lands, untravelled.

One day, we realize that our passions
are substantial as a mountain, potent as a cloud.
Distance, even death, cannot disrupt our loving.

Behind the ridge the twilight sky is pale yellow.
Who knows what darkness will bring?

Made in the USA
Columbia, SC
01 November 2018